Transforming Your Life For 3 Phases, How To Find A Mrs. Smith?

Your Free Gift

I wanted to show my appreciation that you support my work so I've put together a free gift for you.

Just write me letter with this phrase:
«Life as it is»

To mail - Jimmy.white@list.ru

TABLE OF CONTENTS

Introduction

The relationship between the opposite sex is very important, so we live in a society, and we want to enjoy life. Want of socialization.

The authors of this book are several people. Some of them are regular guys who have experienced similar situations and successfully coped with them. As part of this professional psychologists, who have adapted their knowledge, our arguments and thoughts, to avoid misleading the reader.

Dear reader, in this book you will feel yourself in male company, among associates and assistants who understands you like no other.

In this book, we talk about us, and a little about women.

The book is based on explicit experiences of an ordinary guy who fell on it and passed all 3 phases described in this book.

Why us?

Usually immediately after breaking up, we want to be one and not listening to parents, grandparents, friends, etc.

Because they have witnessed your relationship, and perhaps not all approve of your choice.

This problem finds us unawares, and that "its" with the situation takes a while. So we divided this process for days. We hope that this book will replace you with antidepressants.

We are literally the Regent square, the most problematic places, which are trying not to think and afraid to admit it to myself.

For whom is this book?

For guys, men. For those guys who are going through a break-up with a girl and don't know what to do. In this book you will find almost step by step plan for your recovery. Think of this book as a conversation with senior comrades and friends who come for your improvement. I will not give thee perish BRO!

Also, if you want serious and long-standing relationships, this book is also for you.

The book is crammed with different "gimmicks that really work.

The authors decided to explore this issue in some

2

depth and give an integrated permit. So this book is not on the truck!) Is the Pickup you need to approach and meet, and we'll tell you how making yourself this guy to girls themselves acquainted with you.

Unfortunately, just not tell: (in this book. So, if you have any issues in the sphere of relations, contact us via e-mail: Jimmy.white@list.ru

We will try to help you!

What is the value of the book?

The tips in this book are based on real events completed. What we say, every one of us has experienced. Therefore, all our tips really work. Everyone knows that a need to work. In this book, we describe how to work with and cite examples from real life. We'll give you a magic kick in the pants!)

PHASE I

Hit Like A Ton Of Bricks

Before moving to this chapter, I want to talk to you about that why do we need relations with girls. Me personally, it is very important to feel those emotions, which can give a wonderful girl. You are so good and you can! It is the emotions that we experience during sex and eat each others views during sex, while holding her hand. But unfortunately, everything ends up failing to start.

This is only the beginning... This is the most severe stage. We think that the life is finished and we are trying to return something.

I personally have it was so. Met a girl 6 months: all was not bad, often quarreled, but always reconciled. Once again we quarreled, and I saw her eyes went out and changed. I did not understand what was happening. And imagine she already stopped loving me long ago! She said earlier that her right was shaking when she saw me. Some

Brad! Just a nightmare. I really do not understand how a man who today swore me in love, and then just so took and gave. Stay away from these women away. Okay, let's discuss what to do.

Need to analyze calmly, what is the matter. If possible, meet with the girl and talk quietly. Ask why? Let him explain. And then the girls called the different reasons behind which hides a certain meaning.

Here are some common phrases:

1. "I mean, it's not for you, simply, we are different"-most likely you became more interesting and she's tired of you.

2. "Let's be friends"-there is another guy.

3. "I'm not ready for serious relations"-the same.

4. "I'm tired"-you are not interested in it.

In any case, try to find out the real cause of your gap. Not plead and beg, just get the truth. Why do you need to achieve the truth?

I will tell you a story that happened with my friend Fima.

FIMA met a girl 2 years and they really loved each other. But one girl Fima called him and said that everything is over, saying nothing. FIMA didn't realize what happened and wanted to sort out, but failed. Through 6 months after breaking up Lisa's mom called him and said that she died. As it turned out, Lisa had cancer, and she didn't want to Fima suffered. Imagine how he felt? He still blames himself.

So guys, try to find out everything down to the smallest detail. At the last meeting and say what you really feel. If you like, say: "I love you and I don't want to let go, but if you decided-I don't want to persuade you. Because I see that you no longer love me. " If she starts talking, that he loves, but just... (For any reason). Don't listen to just silently leave. Believe me, you'll witness it to be unexpected! It is such from you does not expect exactly. She thinks that controls the situation!)

We consider a situation where the cause of it: tired, it was not fun anymore doesn't love you, there's another. The first thing to do is to accept and never try anything to return. You do not need to score in Google "how to get your favorite. Realize one truth: the girl never you will not abandon and releases, if likes and just thank fate for what you separated from the unnecessary man. Understand and prove to yourself that the reason for it, but not you.

This is very important! So how will affect your self-esteem in the process the following relationships.

The first day is the most complex. You will get sick. Suffer. It will take place. The first time I really helped. There are 2 tracks that I raised and I just nor digicam owner yet to such an extent that I went to the gym, started swinging and running around.

These tracks:

1. **Ice Cube – Gangsta Rap Made Me Do It**

2. **Lil Wayne, Wiz Khalifa & Imagine Dragons w/ Logic & Ty Dolla $ign ft X Ambassadors – Sucker For Pain.**

Take phone, headphones and forward. The idea is to maximally occupy their brains. And the best way to start is to exercise. Go to the mirror and ask yourself: "do I Like myself?" if not, then the output is obvious: you need to go to the gym!

More than useful Hall?

In the Hall so many beautiful girls that they look great and not against. If you can cope with them and a trivial task to some girl just to talk, and then treat her orange frash, get good emotions that would heal your wound.

After meeting hall with friends, if you have them. If you have no friends, go home, shower and lie down to sleep or watch some funny videos on YouTube.

On the next day, try to load itself interesting work. Start planning. You will want to paint your life by hours in the near future. Program your Hydroplane for a weekend meeting with friends (preferably to be among your friends were girls if girls don't have, go with friends in the Club and flirt with beauties).

Sorority you really need now is as close to you was a girl that had feminine energy. And now this power is gone, and you need to replenish stocks). And then you've got to feel attractive to girls. This is very important! And believe me, even your ex-girlfriend is more pleasant to see you in good condition. And no one will believe that she dumped you.

Next, do everything the same: make the sport, keep in touch with friends and family start to plan some interesting things in his life.

This stage takes approximately 1-2 weeks. The objective of this phase: to transform your negative in the right direction. You must understand that everything bad that you have left inside after the departure of the girls, has not disappeared. Negative cannot simply quit. It must be transformed into positive energy, so at this stage it is necessary to maximally exploit yourself in interesting areas of life. It is at this stage that we need to think about yourself. You need to love yourself with renewed vigor. Become for themselves the meaning of life.

About the women at this stage. Now you just need to communicate. Because sex does not abolish all your sadness, but will only aggravate the situation, so don't even think about it.

The ability to forgive

The Council now from our psychologist. To ensure that energy is not upset to the thoughts of the past, you must forgive the past, embrace it. To do this, you need to write with his left hand in the first place, parents and all the people that we have been wronged.

Unknown Yogi good wrote about this: "may the lion's share of your attention is absorbed by the past.

You often say and think about it with bitterness or warmth? You remember their victories, adventures and experiences or imagine himself in the role of victim, endlessly speculating about how you have been treated unfairly or yourself as you have caused someone in pain? What feelings give you these thought processes-guilt, pride, resentment, anger, remorse, self-pity?

In this case, you will not only strengthen its false self-perception, but also encourages physical aging of the body accumulating in its psyche of weight of the past. Something in your past came not as you like, and you still resist what was, and now here is and what resistance is.

However, if you focus the error committed in the past, you start experiencing remorse, blaming himself and struggling with guilt, you turn this error in part yourself, you identify yourself with your past with your mind. Inability to forgive invariably carries a heavy burden of psychological time.

Also, gait and towards his ex-girlfriend, forgive her and wish her all the best mentally. You should be cleansed in order to prepare for the new relationship.

PHASE II

Creation Of A Structure

"Man, as an empty

A vessel that has a rigid structure

that fills a woman."

Buddha

Before seeing his beloved and only woman a man needs to be a structure, that is, his whole life was built:

-Work

-Sport

-Hobby

-Friends

-Life goals.

Later we will describe each element of the structure.

This phase also involves concentration on yourself. At this stage, it is better not to create serious relationships, but to communicate with the girls is a must. That you do not lose the skill of communication. Your life must be filled.

At this point, our brains are more calm and we can enjoy his life more seriously. Where do you start? Of course with itself. There are basic indicators, which draws the attention of virtually all female (polled 10,000 girls in this topic). What do you think, what metrics?

1. Self-confidence

Confidence is how do you feel about humans. You should be comfortable and relaxed. The girls look like you're behaving yourself on people. After all, you'll have to protect her, if that). So calm down and grow in all areas. To feel confident, you gotta look back incredibly keep exactly when gait, behave naturally. Confidence is formed at the expense of the indicators that we will describe below. Try to always be in a good state of mind on the part of it already attracts.

2. Voice

Sometimes, you see an attractive person and think about it well. But it's worth it to talk, as the first impression will be erased instantly! Timbre is very important and it is as you say. Timbre should be nice and low. Such a voice inspires confidence and sexual attraction in the subconscious of the girls.

How to develop a good and steady voice?

Not so difficult, but take some time. There are a number of exercises that you'll find yourself on the Internet. We give here a few interesting chips.

3. Appearance (especially inflated buttocks)

Person:

If you have problems with the face (acne, rashes) try to start eating right.

Teeth:

If there is a problem, then go to the dentist and always keep with me chewing gum. Bad breath very off-putting and even unpleasant.

Hairdresser:

Go to the Barber Shop. Let them pick up a haircut under your hair growth.

Hands:

Nails should be well-groomed.

Legs:

Fingernails should also be well maintained. If your

feet have an unpleasant smell, use deodorant for legs and keep your feet healthy.

The body:

You do not need to be a bodybuilder! Not all strokes love. Just keep yourself in shape, be strong and full of energy. Better make a banner of his body. You need flexibility everywhere). Yoga-for example and some martial arts that can fend for themselves and their loved ones.

Wardrobe:

Try to dress stylishly. Do not need too mannered. Clothing must be clean and pressed. Shoes should be clean and not torn. Watch also for socks and underwear that you dress in the morning. Because you don't know where you find yourself in the evening) (all of a sudden you'll have to get undressed in front of a girl). This is important!

So immediately go and buy yourself a few pairs of good socks and panties.

4. Behavior in humans

You should be friendly with everyone, even with these people. Develop an adequate response in itself: i.e. you are friendly with everyone, but if you need to show aggression to the attacker, you correctly estimate the situation and make the right conclusions.

* Tip: when you walk down the street hold your

back straight and look ourselves in the eye level-
this will understand that confidentiality and not
divorced from reality.

5. View

The view should be purposeful and confident.

*Tip. From Vedic warriors was one exercise that
helped them develop a strong opinion. Take a
candle and light it. See the candle flame closer
until you can. This is a very effective exercise.*

This is to ensure, for example, that when you like
some girl, you look at it without fear, straight in the
eye and not look away.

*Tip. Choose your model and select those traits in
the character, appearance, that you like in a man.
This can be your friend, father, friend or just
famous and successful people. Let's take for
example Jason Statham. I am sure that many
close to the image. Note how he dresses, how
behaves. Make sure its a way of life. And take for
themselves those features that you like and that
you would like to make in your life. It's much
easier than coming up with something new.*

Now let's consider the inner experiences. We have
not forgotten that recently made a mistake and
picked the wrong girl. Therefore, in us all-well,
some uncertainty reigns, which does not normally
deal with cases and live in pleasure.

I solved this problem for yourself.

There is an extra way to deal with their emotions and a longer way.

An emergency way - "Holotropic Breathwork" so-called intensive breath, similar to meditation, through which all fears and worries.

Provoking themselves. Quite a lot of information on the Internet.

Tip: Choose a certified specialist!

A long way. That's already 3 years I practice Chinese martial art "Tai Chi Chuan". That gave me those lessons? I quieted my mind stopped, stopped cheering, became more smiling, strengthened the muscles, ligaments, tendons, became more flexible, learned to move better as in dance, and in battle.

They need to deal with the rest of my life to maintain the normal condition. For the inner workings of this enough.

Now attention! I called you 2 methods that replace:

-Antidepressants;

-Visits to psychologists;

-Any trainings (which does not always help).

Remember! You can help yourself to deal with your inner world.

This is where to start. Find inner peace and the

whole world will be at your feet.

Here are some basic questions that you should answer yourself:

1. I Appreciate himself?

2. I respect myself?

3. What I want in life really?

Write directly in this book answers against those questions. And then, when read this entire book, see if your opinion has changed.

By the way guys can also go on dancing. There's a lot of girls (especially where teach Latin dance-salsa, Bachata). At the same time learn to dance and make themselves more attractive and sexy.

And when you put in order all mentioned above, you should now raise your self-esteem and have fun. How to do it?

Meet beautiful girls, to which perhaps before you were afraid to even approach. Don't be afraid of failure! You're already confident guy. Boldly go and you will see what you're attracting. It's a real thrill when you like beautiful girls. This is very important! Man, it is important to establish themselves in their own eyes, to prove to himself that he can be loved. And when you're chatting and meet such girls, your life will be filled with bright colors and you just forget about the sadness. But at this stage it is important not to relax! Because when we have everything, it turns out, it seems to us that it always will. No!) It will be so only if you are working on a daily basis.

How to get acquainted with these girls?

Not so difficult. For example: go to the largest shopping centre in time period: 12:00-14:00. At this time, usually many business women go for lunch.

Go to the girl you like and start a conversation. You need to start with something in common that unites you. For example: "Girl Hello! You also went out for lunch? Perfectly) Let's have a coffee together. Tell me about your stressful day "or something like that)

Most importantly, be yourself. Do not put your mind at rest, not be obsessed with one girl, just behave decently, but relaxed as if is your longtime girlfriend. Bury rooms, keep in touch with them. In your life should be a lot of beautiful girls with whom you communicate. Not necessarily sleep with them-just communicate well as friends. Your life will be filled this way.

Now let's talk a little about women.

As we have said, at this stage you are not interested in serious relationships. You're busy: develop, you earn money. When you earned some money and you wanted to sex, then don't waste your time dating with women on the street and other nonsense. Go to a good brothel and chose your expensive and beautiful prostitute (unless of course you have 21). Go with her to a restaurant or Café, walk tall. Dear courtesan very smart and educated girls and they look really cute and neat. No one would ever guess that this prostitute. These girls will you listen attentively, smile to you. Imagine that you go just with a very beautiful girl and you all have. Passing the girls will notice you next to a beauty. Girls subconsciously believe that if a guy near some beautiful girl, then it is attractive and you can trust him. Female logic guys!)

Then take this beauty in your hotel or home (preferably). You have a great opportunity to practice their sexual skills. Yes and it is likely that these girls you will learn something too). I have, for example, there are a few familiar expensive prostitutes who call me just like that. They liked to spend time with me and they want me to see for free.

It's such a girl. I want to prove to you that they are even better than regular girls. Attention! We are talking about the benefits of prostitutes precisely at this stage.

In the first place. You do not know well your new friend. You don't know how many guys she had. Don't know whether it occurs with somebody.

Elite prostitute passes permanent medical examination, for her health watch. This is a plus for me.

Secondly. You just know that you will have sex when you want, if you paid the money. You get what you count. With normal girls do not. You can spend a lot of money on it, but can not get not that sex! And even mutual sympathy.

Thirdly. In the morning you can always call her a prostitute taxi. And she left. In my opinion, this is a huge plus.

I hope that nobody is offended in this section. Understand, I'm not pushing prostitution. But at this stage we want sex. And I want to sex with goddesses. With beautiful girls who will we desire. Even for the money! But because we earned them. So we something has succeeded. The more I do not appeal to use the services of any prostitutes. Only the elite and expensive. You always in life meet, such women. At this stage it is very important to start yourself to really appreciate. So, when you feel yourself welcome beautiful girls-do you grow wings. But don't become presumptuous!

Remember! The most important thing in your life is your structure, thanks to which you will be able to create his own family and will be treated as a real man.

Phase III

Build A Serious Relationship

Building relationships

So, dear friend, go to this step, when you successfully passed. Make sure your structure is stable and durable. What is the structure that you have studied in the past section.

Immediately raises a good question: where to go?

If you want a serious and long term relationship, then immediately forget about places such as clubs, dating sites.

It's not serious! Girls from these places where we are interested in past 2-x.

There are 2 ways.

1. 1-trust fate and wait until you'll be surprised)

2. 2-ND-think what you want girl, what criteria should meet (well it certainly figuratively, because the girl is not good).

Ideally, look for a girl among her friends, acquaintances, relatives, former classmates. In a lot of pluses. You already know a lot about his former classmate, and externally they are likely to have changed for the better.

When you meet the girl of your dreams, you cannot disable the brain!)

The first time-this time, love, and nothing we understand, we just like everything in a girl. But it's a trap! Remember in the first phase of the relationship we are attentive to the girl and maximally soberly assess the candidate on your wife.

The most important thing is to see how a girl behaves in humans, with your friends.

Tip: Invite her to meet friends and girlfriends. Enjoy and watch carefully how behaves girl. It relaxes and begin to behave as she wants. And you look if you want to see such a girl.

It's cool! Let's say a girl behaves decently and properly, even being in the intoxication with your friends.

Let your girl will acquaint you with their friends and girlfriends. You need to know to whom your girl because the girlfriend has a big impact. And in the early stages is very important, like her girlfriends. Because she knows more than you) So that a friend at a meeting with her friends be polite and considerate as much as possible, even if you didn't like her girlfriends).

Also pay attention to what does your girl about her ex, criticizes or berates whether someone from strangers. This is very important, because what if it said about his former, means she has some feelings for him. This can be a problem for your further relations.

In the early stages of your relationship, plan their time correctly. Don't sacrifice your deeds for the sake of it. (Exception: if she needed help and if it sacrifices for you). And here's dear friend, we reached to the main question: How do I know that the girl is right for you at first sight?

Should be the impact of girls! What does this mean? This kind of initiative from its sides, for example: she first called you, when you're sitting in a cafe she gave you a napkin to you wiped his own mouth. It shows what a good girl. And this kindness sincere that she was unconscious and conscious.

The girl must be good. It's still the expectant mother of your children. So pay attention to this factor.

For example, suppose your girl fits all of these criteria.

The following object for study: both of her parents.

This is a very important factor, because you want to see which family relations respected their father how is mother. Your girl has a certain model of her family in which she lives.

Tip. Tell a girl that she introduced you to her parents. Prepare for an appointment: buy mother flowers, father-something interesting (depending on what he likes). Try at the meeting not to drink: you must evaluate the situation as much as possible and understand everything good in your family girl.

Believe me, each girl's family is very important. My friends and I have repeatedly made mistakes when choosing a girl because ignored such an important factor as the girl's parents.

The ideal situation: the father and the mother of your girls, live together, love each other, respect each other. But if everything is bad, don't go throw your girl. Talk to her: maybe she wants in her family, everything was different.

Further, you can introduce her to his parents. Carefully listen to what she has to say about your loved ones after meeting with them. Remember! If a girl bad said about your loved ones-this is a bad sign. You need to think about.

Then arrange vacations you with a girl and your parents. You should see how they will get along with each other. Ideally, leave nature somewhere where you'll be away from home.

If the girl and her parents passed this test successfully, then this is a good sign, but don't relax.

At this stage you must have money to afford to live separately from their parents with a girl.

Here the fun begins

You must configure correctly, your life. Many girls afraid to live for the first time with a guy, because you need to Cook, wash clothes, clean the apartment or House. But it's not scary) Talk with his girlfriend and explain to her that since you switched to a more serious level of relationship, you will plan and build a home life.

* Tip. Stick to the basic rules of living together with the girl.

Don't make her Cook

In General, usually if a girl likes you, she will cook for you even if you do not know-learn. So it all depends on the girl. But if a girl does not prepare, but you want to try to cook together for a while. If she likes it, she herself starts to cook for you.

Do surprises

Joint life should not become a routine. Girls can not stand this. So don't wait motives and Dari flowers, small gifts, which would lift the mood of your girlfriend. Remember! You want to be interesting and not predictable (your girl will love you even more). So girls that are arranged in the first stages of the relationship need to motivate them and intrigue that they did not know about your next step. And then you deserve true love. Consider this your profitable investment in your happy relationship.

Do housework together

Choose day and time, for example-Saturday, to make all accumulated routine housework together.

Firstly, together able to work faster.

Secondly-in this lesson, you will bring.

After work necessarily invite a girl somewhere to go, so she knew that for this work, she will receive good emotions and a surprise from you.

So the girl gets tired mentally and be in a good mood.

Be the best lover

Sex is no less important in your life. Here of course everything depends on the capabilities of your little another.

But there is something that is capable of every prelude. This is a very important part of sex, so don't ignore this, even if you're a sex giant!)

Be gentle and do not hurry. Saw a girl how beautiful she is and welcome you. Slowly razdevaj her, do her Kiss compliments, gently smooth surface.

Excite her to the limit and then you are significantly zooming their chances to meet.

Spend most of their free time together.

Friends is a good thing. But need to find classes that are interesting to you too. For example: you can travel together. This fun and useful. You can, however, engage in sports.

Spend time in common companies your friends. Let your separate leisure an exception!)

Be an example in everything

The girl needs you to believe and listen to your opinion. For this you need to keep your Word and always do what promise. Clear?! This is very important.

Your task in the early stages of dating and living together deserve the compliments from the girls. When a girl will respect you, then she will be honest with you, and would you believe. It is the Foundation of any relationship.

Never beat girl!

It so happens that the girl is very annoying and it makes you want to hit. Better go away. Outside and cool off. Later pairs. And then start to communicate.

Remember: as soon as you hit a woman, you lost her respect forever.

After a quarrel explain girl that during quarrels you better not touch. If she does not want you specifically anger, she will understand you and make everything right.

Correct build relations with their parents and the parents of the girl.

Girls often envy us-guys to our parents (especially mothers). Girls love also implicate us in their conflicts with their parents. Clearly separate your relationship with the girl and your relationship with your parents. To the girl was jealous of your mother - don't let her motives. For example: If the girl will cook something for your total dinner, praise her and say that this is the most delicious that you've ever eaten. The first time your girlfriend need to show that you are one family and the cause for jealousy not. And you will see how after a while your girlfriend and your mom will be best friends!

A separate place still wanted to highlight for romance. We'll show you one chip you might practice itself, but still look.

In the early stages of your new girl for sure will appreciate this gesture.

Find out where your girl and prepare for her

romantic letter. Below we have provided for you one of our letters written for girls.

Was it in the romantic style. Write a letter to her.

I'm now going to show you one ideal model of relations, which is the most durable and accurate. My friends and I live in this model.

You're the man, Chief in the family. You have a good job, you are able to provide for his family. Your wife does not work, but she has a hobby that it brings money (for example: she is a photographer, Designer). Your wife greets you after work, feeds you delicious, wondered how do you day.

You bring her flowers, doing surprises. You are travelling together and spend most of their free time together. It respects your parents and never talks about them is bad. You have children, you love and grow in a healthy environment. You did not smoke did not drink, lead a healthy lifestyle.

Rules for family life

In order to achieve greater success in life, in family relationships should be respected the following seven rules.

1. Enthusiasm. This ability to perform their duties with joy. Perhaps it is only when the family has a serious purpose. The goal means communication with something. Suppose we are tied to a purpose that brings us happiness. People, for example, believe in God or are self-aware. If a family has a

very serious goal, it is happiness. If the goal is not that severe, it bears the only problem.

So when people pose a serious purpose, they naturally appear enthusiastic for her accomplishments as they are communicating with this end, to receive from her force happiness.

Thus, the enthusiasm is the first necessity of life. Enthusiasm brightens up all family problems and enables people to live with each other, even if they do not have sufficient compatibility or they misunderstand each other in any issues.

2. Vera. People who are married, have throughout, fully trusted each other. Must be the belief that a person inclined to sacrifice themselves for the sake of you, in fact, that he is faithful to you.

If there is such a belief, it is possible to act honestly, openly, straight-life does not become političnoj, indirect, dry.

3. Patience. Patience means understanding that man can not be changed in one second, and generally it is very difficult to change.

Therefore, if you have tied your life with this person, you must go to any concessions. In this case, patience means concessions-giving person to be wrong.

4. Compliance with the rules. It is necessary to choose the laws according to which a family lives, such as Vedic principles and strictly follow them.

Depending on your views on life, you can take a Muslim, Christian principles and so on. Action on the basis of these principles is the key to success. Sometimes between husband and wife there are disagreements, but if they believe in any rules, build their lives based on certain principles, it may find the answer to your questions in one way or another Scripture. In this case, all disputes are solved-just to Scripture in the family were common.

5. The family must also desist from communicating with degraded personalities that bring big concern family life.

6. The following very important rule-people must deal with self-awareness, that is, as we have said, there must be some purpose in life. Without such objective family can spend time in vain and then family members easily appear bad habits. These bad habits will lead to a very big problem. Also, without practice self-awareness necessarily cause problems in the relationship between the spouses and child-rearing.

7. The fact is that the relationship of man and woman except that bring pleasure to both still have negative sides. When close communion with men a woman

if a man will not have any purpose in life, he will inevitably overly attached to a woman, since it is always more pleasant to communicate with a close friend, rather than something to worry about. And overcome the cravings for the opposite sex any idea or desire in life quite difficult. We know very many examples from history and from life when very serious people, aspiring to something great or sublime, forget about all the Bewitched women's charms.

Also in the family, when a man strongly attached to his wife and children, regardless of their it will mentally weaken. All his interests to roll family problems. But a man primarily valued for its ability to achieve something big. It is only natural that women appreciate men for money, for their respect in society, etc. But to achieve such success in the life of man is capable of when he gently tied to women or to the family comfort. Moreover, most women are attracted to a man the ability not to be involved in their beauty and charm. When a woman sees a man, she feels that it is a very serious man, and was to him a great deal of respect and a desire to somehow be useful, to be under its the protection.

In addition, the husband for the wife becomes naturally very costly if it fulfilled all its responsibilities and takes care of the family, but not much of it is waiting for some benefits, respect or caress. Such a State of man could not develop artificially. It comes to a man automatically, if it is seriously engaged in self-awareness, trying to grasp its spiritual nature. If man is reasonable, then he will be able to arrange their lives so that the practice of self-awareness does not disturb the material side of life. But you also need to learn.

With such a lifestyle man becomes capable of more sober relate to the opposite sex, but this does not mean that he becomes insensitive, cold, mad or impotent. He just becomes able to properly control their feelings and motivations, manifests the real spiritual power of men.

Thus, a family man must take responsibility for his wife, children and their families who are in need of support. Ownership does not mean that the head of the family considers itself completely around the right and disposes of all as wants or what he earned money, and the rest can relax in a family atmosphere. Responsibility means that a man takes care of all family members in all respects: physical, moral and moral-care to all members of the family were busy with their affairs properly according to their abilities, to keep them happy in life and do not engage in useless adverse for other causes and not catapulted into harmful habits. Taking responsibility, stated in the Vedas, makes people happy, because the attitude is very much changing for the better.

The key to a successful life!

PROACTIVE LIFE benefit life proactive implies that you must act proactively with respect to any aspect of life.

If you want to get married or get married, you should begin to prepare for this for several years: read the relevant literature, learning how to achieve harmony in family life, as find a partner that suits you, etc.

If you want to enroll in some kind of institution, start learning new subjects, the training should begin at least a year. You must understand why you need it, whether this study, your nature, your mission and purpose of life.

The same with food-it should be treated carefully. You can, of course, there are on the move, for 5 minutes, without focusing on the process of eating, but it leads to diseases and nervous system arousal. Better to sit quietly, to pray, to give the process of eating for a while, but do it w goodness. With nutrition starts very much. If you eat right, stay in his goodness will always much easier.

Sleep is also very important. We always have some kind of case, and go to 10-11 pm elusive. So goes the day after day, year after year, and it has a negative impact on our health. Initially heavily accustom yourself to go to bed early, the mind tries to find excuses: "but all impose a late..."but if you have a strong desire to do it-you'll see that everything will change, and even your relatives somehow begin to fall before.

With regard to work, people often complain that they work hard, they don't appreciate, not increase. But these people who are regularly engaged in self-education? According to statistics obtained by American researchers, if you at least an hour a day doing self-education in his specialty, read relevant books or articles on the Internet, visit courses of qualification improvement, etc., there is a very powerful energy of success and unexpected things start to happen: you suddenly increase, are invited to work in a forward-looking company you want an interesting project. But for this purpose, it is necessary to act proactively-that's exactly what all successful people.

Self-education in ignorance: people prone to frequent viewing TV, play computer games, abounding with aggression, violence and sex, live in a dirty House or apartment. Reading as a habit or no, or only on the above topics.

There is confidence: Why teach me something I did and so all know and can teach others to himself. "Look at the book and see..." This expression for those in the character dominated by passion and ignorance.

Self-education in passion (Rajas)- bad man concentrates, often distracted by something else, or, for example, five hours continuously learn something and then two weeks off.

All study questions related to how to earn more money, improve your sex life and physical beauty, how to better manipulate people, etc. A better deal for half an hour a day, but do it regularly, then it will be training in genuine goodness. It is thus advised, for example, to teach foreign languages.

Productivity initially requires a certain effort has a good phrase: "Diamond turns out from constant pressure. But under the pressure of the supply voltage is not passion. It is important to do something always and maintain this status. Constancy and maintenance-these two words belong to the guna goodness. Skill produced at the repeated repetition of an action.

For example, getting up early in the morning. At first it is difficult. People who have a little solar power, tend to get up late. People categorized as "OWL" uptime is increased only in the evening.

Conclusion

Here's our conversation came to an end. I hope you have already realized that your life belongs to you and you build your life. You also understand that this process takes some time, you should spend usefully.

This brief tutorial is as intensive, with which you must read and understand the key direction. In more detail with each step you will see the following books where we meet with each step in detail. So keep an eye out for our new products and announcements.

Good Luck BRO! We are always nearby.

Insert chapter one text here. Insert chapter one text here. Insert chapter one text here. Insert chapter one text here. Insert chapter one text here. Insert chapter one text here. Insert chapter one text here. Insert chapter one text here. Insert chapter one text here. Insert chapter one text here. Insert chapter one text here.

www.ingramcontent.com/pod-product-compliance
Lightning Source LLC
Chambersburg PA
CBHW070237290526
45789CB00004B/1660